THE QUANTOCKS
ON ENGLISH HILLS

The Life and the Land

G.J. Penny

Somerset Books in association with

First published in Great Britain in 2004

Title page image: *Round up of the commoners' sheep at Halsway Post, 2002*

British Library Cataloguing-in-Publication Data
A CIP record for this title is available from the British Library

ISBN 0 86183 412 7

SOMERSET BOOKS
Somerset Book is a partnership between DAA Halsgrove Ltd and Somerset County Council (Directorate of Culture and Heritage)
www.somerset.gov.uk

Halsgrove House, Lower Moor Way, Tiverton EX16 6SS
T: 01884 243242 F: 01884 243325
e: sales@halsgrove.com w: www.halsgrove.com

Printed and bound by D'Auria Industrie Grafiche Spa, Italy

A selection of Gary's work from this title and other projects can be found at www.wessexfoto.com

To Jacki and Guy,
without whom the struggle would not have been worth it.

To all the people of the Quantock Hills who appear in these images I give my warm thanks. I must also say a hearty thank you to Andrew Snell and his staff at London Camera exchange in Taunton, Chas Halsey and the team at Focal Point in Exeter, and all at Mifsud Photographic in Brixham, for their generosity, patience and good will. Most of all I want to say thank you to my GP, Dr Catherine Fenlon, to my Oncologist Dr Chris Price, and all the staff at the Bristol Royal Infirmary, especially the oncology nurses of ward 61, and to my surgeon, Mr John Dixon, and all the nurses at Southmead Hospital, Bristol. It is fair say that without the hard work and tough love of these people this book would, quite literally, have never happened.

Rock Farm, Bagborough

'Trackway and camp and city lost
salt marsh where now is corn
old wars, old peace
old arts that cease
and so was England born'

Kipling

Introduction

This work grew, in part, from a conversation with Iain Porter, projects officer of the Quantock Hills Area of Outstanding Natural Beauty, about the importance of putting together into an archive the images I had begun to take of the people and places around the hill. Without the A.O.N.B. service's practical and financial support over the last two years, this work would not have been possible. The idea is to have this archive, based at the offices of the A.O.N.B., as a resource of images which can help to build a picture of the lives of the people of this small corner of Somerset at the beginning of this new millennium. The value of an archive like this is not in the dramatic or the picturesque, but in those small, and sometimes unnoticed parts of our ordinary daily lives which help to define who we are.

I have found the people of this small corner of England to be unfailingly generous with their time, and open in allowing me access to photograph their lives. The great joy in making these pictures has been the chance to meet so many interesting people. What these people have in common is that they are all part of the community of the Quantock Hills. There is something about these hills which seem to draw you to them, a sense of place, and of timelessness. In many ways the Quantock Hills are the poor relations to their nearest neighbour Exmoor. Being smaller than Exmoor and yet so near, many visitors drive along the A39 coast road on their way further west, without stopping to discover the simpler, perhaps less commercialised joys of the Quantocks. These hills can boast great views across the Severn estuary to Wales, many historic and picturesque villages, ancient trees, and abundant wildlife. As well as being England's first designated Area of Outstanding Natural Beauty, these hills are home to one of England's three packs of stag hounds. The deer are (rather surprisingly to some) an introduced species. They were introduced to give sport for nineteenth century landowners. Visitors love to see them on the hill but farmers are less inclined to suffer them eating their crops. Many put up with it only because of the benefits the hunt brings – one of which is the removal of dead animals from farms by the hunt, which then uses the carcasses to feed the hounds. In addition, in my personal experience the meetings of the hunt are hugely warm social gatherings, where people of all age groups gather together to enjoy each other's company, make and remake old acquaintances, swap news and relax. It is hard not to see these multigenerational gatherings as almost unique in our society today. The irony though, is that a total ban on hunting with hounds may well bring about the complete demise of deer on the hill as farmers on and around the hill refuse to accept the destruction to their crops, without the associated benefits the hunt brings both commercially and socially.

Summer fêtes always seem to bring out the best in people. Whether it be in the produce competition, or the beer tent, these rural fêtes offer rich pickings for the observer of humankind. Likewise the many horse shows and gymkhanas which take place each year give young and not so young riders a chance to compete for the much coveted rosettes.

In the town of Williton, there is a firm which locally at least is almost an institution – J. Gliddon & Sons. Founded in 1833, Gliddon's is where you go to buy, well, just about anything you can think of actually. If it's a new tractor you're after, or a pair of new wellies, or perhaps, you need one of those widget things that goes on the end of the flange wotsit, then you'll find it in the the ironmonger's shop. Here nails can still be bought by weight in paper bags, not pre-packed and vacuum sealed a half dozen at a time! What really drew me to Gliddon's was the length of time most of the staff have been there. I went to take a picture of Ray Long who was leaving to retire after twenty-four years, to discover that, far from being unusual, he had in fact been there half as long as the longest serving member of staff, and that James (the new boy) had been with the firm for five years! In an age when we are encouraged to think that jobs for life are a thing of the past, there are still firms which can set value on loyalty.

There are other gems to be found, when you take the time to look, like Triscombe Nursery, where plants are still more important than coffee shops and nick nacks, and the staff can give you real advice. And if you ask really nicely, the owner might give you a tour of his arboretum, and let you admire his wrought iron stag.

I don't want you to get the wrong idea: these hills have their share of modern life too. Tucked away at the north west end at West Quantoxhead is St Audries Park; once a private dwelling it later became a private girls' school, and is now a dedicated wedding venue. Here the modern bride (now on average in her mid thirties) can have the wedding of her dreams. Gone are the days of paper table cloths and plastic knives. Today's brides arrive in horse drawn carriages, vintage cars or even helicopters, and plans for the day are often made years in advance. Fewer and fewer of these couples are including a religious element in their big day and, as they will be footing the bill themselves, they get what they want. For many years, country house hotels have offered themselves as wedding venues. What makes places like St Audries Park different, is that they are not hotels, but dedicated wedding providers.

As our countryside is made more open to the public, we have to acknowledge the work done by a devoted band of often overlooked workers, the rangers and wardens of the Area of Outstanding Natural Beauty, and the National Trust respectively, who work hard to maintain the environment we enjoy. Without burning back the heather to promote healthy new growth (swaling), or bird ringing, or taking school parties on educational trips to teach appreciation of and respect for the countryside and its inhabitants, and the many other tasks they undertake, it is certain this place would be worse off. The word that keeps coming back to me again and again is symbiosis; each of these elements works together to create a sense of place, of community tied in some way to the land, not necessarily 'off' the land, but certainly, true to it.

About my photography

My interest as a photographer is in the social fabric of England and how it defines us. As a photographer, my inspiration comes from the work of the great social documentarians of the twentieth century and the mass observation movement more generally. I have set out to photograph the everyday things around me, the mundane, and even the banal. For those that are interested in the technical details, in my documentary work I use only 35mm film cameras, mainly Nikon SLR's, with either 50mm, 35mm, or 24mm prime lenses. I have been using these cameras for twenty-two years, so old habits die hard. And I try always to remember the advice of the late Robert Capa, 'if your pictures aren't good enough, it's because you're not close enough.' Most of these images of people, were taken within 3 feet of the subject, with either the 35mm or 24mm lens. When you are very close to your subject, close enough to see into their eyes, you have to be communicating with them; taking pictures that capture life requires you to be experiencing it yourself. These pictures are therefore consensual – although we speak of 'taking' pictures, they have in fact been 'made', made in this case with the full participation of the people of the Quantock Hills. I hope you enjoy looking at them as much as I enjoyed making them.

Derelict pole barn, Bagborough

Our English Arcadia

Early morning mist from Bagborough Hill

Quantock beeches

Visitors touring the hill by mountain bike

Tim Russell, senior Quantock ranger

The gates of Crowcombe Court

Cothelstone Manor

Road sign at Crowcombe Heathfield

Ramblers on the cliff top at Kilve

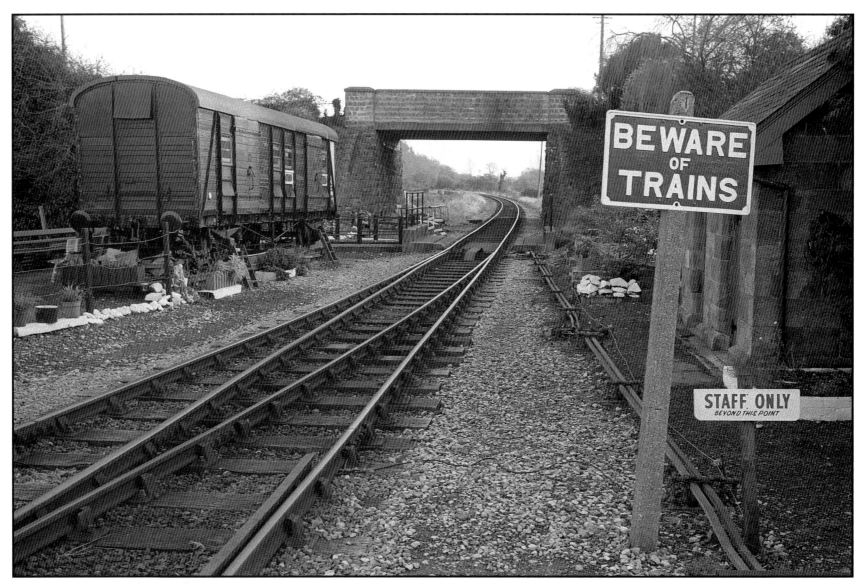

The West Somerset Railway, Williton Station

Crowcombe Heathfield Station in winter

Kilve beach

Ramblers resting on Cothelstone Hill

Road signs at Lydeard Cross

Six serious mountain bikers, at Robin Uprights Hill

Crowcombe church house

War memorial and church house

24

West Somerset Railway at Crowcombe Heathfield

The top of the old steeple which was brought down in a storm in 1725, in Crowcombe churchyard

Grave stones in Crowcombe churchyard

English Heritage surveyors at Dead Woman's Ditch

Popham Hall, Bagborough, on polling day

Old greenhouse at Cothelstone Manor

Cottage gate at Nethercott

Ruined cob barn on the Triscombe road, Bagborough

The gate house at Cleeve Abbey

'Thank him who isled us here, and roughly set
his Briton in blown seas and stormy showers'

Tennyson

Maureen and Dawn, custodians of Cleeve Abbey

Doorway at Cleeve Abbey

Mick 'Prickles' Thorne

Brother and sister share a laugh, outside Gliddon's in Williton

The Golden Jubilee garden party at Crowcombe Heathfield, 2002

Jubilee party

Games at the Jubilee party

Enjoying a laugh

Travelling police unit at Crowcombe Post Office

Heather the Post Mistress at Lydeard St Lawrence

Golden Jubilee at the Carew Arms, Crowcombe, 2002

Mick and Roger at Flaxpool Garage

The travelling library

Parents watching at Saturday morning football club at Crowcombe

Old soldiers. Remembrance service at West Quantoxhead

Paying their respects at Crowcombe

Halsway Manor, home of English song and dance

Halsway Manor from the old gates

Cliff Branson BEM, *and some of the staff of Halsway Manor*

Sir Walter Luttrell, outside Court House, his family's home since 1086

The Crowcombe Golden Jubilee fête 2002

'Her sights and sound, dreams happy as her day: and laughter,
learnt of friend and gentleness in hearts at peace, under an English heaven.'

Brooke

Local ladies selling bric-a-brac

Checking out the produce in the marquee

Sponges in the stocks

Drum group entertaining the fête

Giving out the prizes

Sampling the beer

Bagborough village fête, 2003

New arrivals

Local ladies selling vegetables

Shade on a hot day at Bagborough 2003

The raffle at Sampford Brett

Dr Jazz, the good time band!

Richard Down, Quantock Stag Hounds' huntsman,
showing stag hounds at Bagborough fête

Sampford Brett church on day of the village fête, 2004

Watchet town crier welcoming visitors at Sampford Brett fête, 2004

Tea and cake at the fête

Separating the commoners' sheep at Holford in heavy rain

'Bold immortal country whose hilltops
have stood stronghold for the high gods when
on earth they go, terror for fat burghers in far plains below'

Robert Graves

Nick Gibbons of Staple Farm

Hugh Warmington talking to Mike Langdon at Cothelstone Farm

Cothelstone church, from the farm

Tobie Osmond, the market chaplain

Farmers at Taunton Market

Taunton Market

Anthony Salvage trying to stay dry at the sheep round up

Penning the sheep

Merlin Waygood of Rock Farm

An unconventional kennel

*Michael Branfield using
a chainsaw to lay hedge*

Laying hedges at Crowcombe Heathfield

Mary Hobhouse at her eighteenth-century lambing shed

Moving the new lambs

Janet White, Quantock commoner, feeding sheep by quad bike

Janet White explaining to the author how to tell a Quantock pony from an Exmoor pony

Mick (Prickles) and Pete Thorne
at Higher Aisholt Farm

Viewing at the annual pony sale, London Farm, Bagborough, 2003

Geese at the pony sale

One man and his goose

Auction of tack at the pony sale

The rangers' old Land Rovers on Great Hill

'Grey recumbent tombs of the dead in desert places, standing
stones on the vacant, wine red moor, hills of sheep and the howes
of silent vanished races, and winds, austere and pure'

R. L. Stevenson

Forestry Commission and Quantock AONB staff outside
the Carew Arms, Crowcombe after Ella Briens' leaving party

Andy Harris, Quantock ranger advising the public about rights of way

Iain Porter (Quantock officer) leads a party of school children from Lydeard St Lawrence on a nature ramble on Cothelstone Hill

School trip on Cothelstone Hill

Ella Briens and Andy Harris at Crowcombe Park Gate

Andy Harris, bruising the bracken to discourage future growth at Crowcombe Park Gate

Removing a boulder from the blades of the bruiser

Nigel Garnsworthy, NT warden, and Julien Brooks, volunteer warden, swaling on Great Hill

Tim Russell (fire chief!) hard at work, swaling on the hill

Swaling on Great Hill with National Trust staff

Kevin Godfrey putting signage on Andy Harris's new vehicle

Andy Harris, Nicola Penn, and Doug Miller bird ringing, at sessile oak wood

Wing of young blue tit

Andy Harris with young blue tit

Ella Briens feeding Quantock ponies and cattle on Cothelstone Hill on her
last day with the AONB before moving on to become a Dartmoor ranger

Ella and thoroughbred Exmoor ponies

Tim Russell, Nigel Garnsworthy, Roly Ford, Andy Harris
and Julien Brooks after swaling on Great Hill

Harbouring – looking for deer for that day's hunt

*'And still when mob or monarch lays, too rude a hand on English ways,
the whisper wakes the shudder plays across the reeds at Runnymede'*

Kipling

Humane killers

Meat to feed the hounds

Huntsman and whipper-in working at the kennels

Whipper-in, and Huntsman

Removing a dead cow to be rendered as feed for the hounds

Getting ready at the hunt kennel

*Huntsman, Richard Down
at a Crowcombe meet, 2004*

Feeding the followers

The Quantock Stag Hounds' puppy show, 2002

Advice from an old hand

Following the hunt at Crowcombe Park Gate

Kaaren's spuds

Jamie cadging a lift

Sharing a drink

Liberty Bells

A widely held view?

Boxing Day meet at the Carew Arms, 2002

Leaving the kennels

First ride with the Quantock Stag Hounds

Father and son, waiting for the coach on the day of the Liberty and Livelihood march, 2002

Hunt followers at Adscombe

Young competitor taking time out to watch the opposition

'What is life if, full of care, we have no time to stand and stare.'

W. H. Davies

Waiting to start her round

The secretary's office

Commentary box

The Quantock Show, 2002

Fifth place rosette

Waiting to start

Optimistic mini!

Keen competitors

Having a laugh

Kissing the clown

*Workshop entrance from the auction field. Gliddon & Sons of Williton,
agricultural engineers and ironmongers, are a local institution*

'I desire to leave the men who come after me a remembrance in good works.'

Alfred the Great

The ironmonger's store

The new boy James, only five years at Gliddon's

Workshop manager Clive Rayson – the magic wand is for emergency use only

The general office

Lois Cope, agricultural stores and clothing

Canteen with wall art!

The clock

Wendy on the 'phone in the shop

Fixing a lawnmower

The old till and the new (ish)

Tractor with puncture

Ray Long on his last day, after twenty-four years at Gliddon's ironmongers

Tina Welch arriving at St Audries

'a wise women never yields by appointment'

Stendhal

Church at St Audries

Before the marriage

Horse and carriage used in the BBC TV production of Pride and Prejudice

Before going in to the marriage room

Denise's shoes

American bride, Denise Hagley getting ready for her wedding

St Audries House, West Quantoxhead, 2003 –
fashionable scene of many a Quantock wedding

Bride and bridesmaid

Denise and her mother arriving at the church

'Our England is a garden, and such gardens are not made by singing:
"Oh how beautiful" while better men than we go out and start their working
lives, at grubbing weeds from gravel paths with broken dinner knives.'

Kipling

Stuart Parkman and Andy Harris with iron stag in Stuart's arboretum, Triscombe Nursery

Jonathan Clothier

One of the old greenhouses

Old glass house

Soft fruit, soft signs

Triscombe Nursery staff

Stuart Parkman, nurseryman